The

Universal Guide

to

Running for Office

By: Park Cannon

Note: The following book is designed to give information on running for state-level office.

The purpose of this book is to educate, inspire, and entertain. The author and Clyde Publishers shall have neither liability nor responsibility to any person or entity with respect to any loss or damage caused or alleged to have been caused, directly or indirectly, by the information contained in this book.

Consult an attorney for information on all legal matters.

Printed in the United States of America

Edited By:

Elizabeth Clyde (My God Sister and BFF)

<u>Dedication</u>

To: Mommie, Daddy, and Ross

I am the person I am because of your love and support.

My gratitude extends from Georgia to Chicago through New York City to Vermont because I am wherever you are.

Thank you for instilling patience, hard work, compassion, and determination in my leadership.

My moxie comes from y'all!

Love,

Park

If you plan on running for office, you want it to be one of the most <u>impactful</u> moments of your existence.

The matters are serious, but the goal is to *have fun* while we change the world for the better.

I hope you can enjoy my playlist that I listen to while canvassing with my team.

These 24 songs keep me energized and remind me why I ran for office at age 24:

To serve and to see a better world.

Park's Political Playlist

1. **Ain't No Stopping Us Now** by McFadden and Whitehead
2. **All For You** by Janet Jackson
3. **Blessings on Blessings** by Anthony Brown
4. **Can't Nobody Hold Me Down** by Diddy
5. **Crazy Classic Life** by Janelle Monae
6. **Entrepreneur** by Jay-Z ft. Pharrell
7. **Fight the Power** by Public Enemy
8. **Human Nature** by Madonna
9. **Level Up** by Ciara
10. **Mood 4Eva** by Beyonce
11. **My Vote Don't Count** by Yellopain
12. **Never Too Much** by Luther Vandross
13. **One Of My Favorite Prayers** by Dalai Lama
14. **Pants On the Ground** by Larry Platt
15. **Positions** by Ariana Grande
16. **Pride to the Polls** by The Reps ft. Park Cannon
17. **September** by Earth Wind & Fire
18. **Smile** by Kirk Franklin
19. **Strength, Courage and Wisdom** by India Arie
20. **Toast** by Koffee
21. **Twelve (12) Problems** by Rapsody
22. **We Are One** by MAZE ft. Frankie Beverly
23. **What's Going On** by Marvin Gaye
24. **Work** by Rihanna

***

At the conclusion of this book there is a 120-day affirmation journal that I invite you to join me on!

Legislative session in my state begins the second Monday in January and goes for about 4 months, which equals around 120 days.

In numerology, 120 represents that with creativity and communication, all will turn out for the highest good.

Many campaigns are separated by primary and general elections, which also are about 120 days apart.

If you are interested in working with me as a political consulting client, I consult all the time!

All political consultations involve a one-hour strategy session with myself and a member of my team. I even offer a monthly P.I.P class which is political interview preparation!

Reach out via ParkCannonConsulting@gmail.com

I'd be delighted to be a part of your story!

Table of Contents

1

What does it take?

**"You don't make progress by standing on the
sidelines, whimpering, and complaining.
You make progress by implementing ideas."
~Shirley Chisholm~**

If you have bought this book, it means you are

either considering running for office or

are already doing so.

Make this **your decision** and something that you

have made up your mind to do.

Start by owning the belief that you are qualified to

run for office and that you are committed to this

being your own decision.

It will be imperative that you return to the reasons

supporting **your decision** to run for office,

and for me it was:

1. My family supported me.

2. My community asked me.

January 11, 2021

6:30 AM

Ms. Park Cannon

Call me she and her. Which pronouns do you use?

I am writing this to you after returning from a brisk

walk with my Yorkie pup, Congress.

It is a great morning in Georgia because today is the

first day of the legislative session!

It is a sincere honor to serve in my elected position.

Many of the voters who support me have watched

me and prayed for me to win each of my elections.

I do not take for granted my leadership role and I

have been serving the Old Fourth Ward community

and surrounding areas of the Georgia House of

Representatives' District 58 since I was **twenty-four**.

I was attracted to my seat after a fire was lit

inside of me upon hearing the verdict of

Michael Brown's case.

With a burning desire to bring change to not

just The South, but throughout the world, I sat on

the steps of the Georgia State Capitol and made a

promise to myself.

I told myself that I would make plans to join

the political process as a decision maker, thought

leader, and ultimately a world changer.

I did not exactly know where to begin, but the flame for change was ignited.

I simply started by serving local organizations in my community.

Then one day, as if God were saying I was ready, the graceful Simone Bell called me about vacating her seat.

With a true desire to present my campaign entitled:

Better Solutions For a Better Georgia

I could not think of a better mentor to be supported by than Simone Bell.

#MentorsMatter

I remain grateful to her and all the voters in Georgia that believe in progress for all...

And I cannot deny the forward force of such a powerful decision to **be** the change I wished to see.

I am here to guide you in the best way possible to succeed in politics, but also in your own personal life.

I am no different from you: a girl with parents who love her, a brother she admires, and friends that are my own personal heroes, and **still** I took the political plunge.

Make no mistake, after deciding to run, it was not easy.

I went into four back-to-back elections with contenders.

The 2020 election was the first time I was on the ballot without an opponent.

Having successfully won all four of my elections before I turned 30, I have recognized the depth of my knowledge based on the leadership courses I have completed (Hey, Harvard Kennedy School!), the trainings that I have led (VoteRunLead!) and the multiple positions that I have secured such as Chair, Co-Chair, and Secretary to name a few.

I want you to join me in bringing change to **your** community, city, state, and ultimately the world.

If I could begin this book with one single motivation for you, it is to: **prove them wrong.**

I do not know who your "them" is, but they are not what is most important.

If you now have a desire to speak for anyone in a position of need then now is your time.

Many of us know what it is like for our voices or stories not to be heard. It is time for yours and this is likely why you are reading this book.

Do yourself a favor, and do not run from the call of liberty, we must keep the torch burning.

It is time to get busy!

Let's start by identifying why you want to run for office.

The journey is empowering, yet also isolating due to the nature of the political arena.

We must be clear on our why and always come back
to revisit our purpose when we feel overwhelmed.

**My why was to address community pain and
bring better healthcare access.**

Q&A to Ponder with Park!

1. Are you able to maintain integrity under pressure?

   _____

2. Do you recognize yourself as a change agent in your community?

   _____

3. The bright lights are hot, can you handle being misunderstood?

   _____

4. Are you able to present ideas of others even when you do not necessarily agree with their perspective?

   _____

5. Do you believe that political parties should be able to work together for the greater good of all despite different beliefs?

   _____

Running for office ultimately takes being a voice for others, while also taking on the responsibility of remaining composed even when under attack.

What is your why?

_____

_____

_____

You have what it takes.

Now, let us start adding people to your team!

#TeamWorkMakesTheDreamWork

2

Kitchen Cabinet

"Effective leaders must be truth seekers, and that requires a willingness to understand truths other than our own."
~Stacey Abrams~

You are developing your core team in this stage.

But there is one step I need you to do before we go

into who you need to help you.

Find out what paperwork and forms need to be

filled out for your political committee.

I recommend reaching out to your city clerk, the

state elections division, the county elections board,

and the nearby banks.

Remember, at the city clerk's office there are valuable

resources that may be beneficial to your grassroots

canvassing.

Here is a tip:

When you speak to the election's division, do your

best to find one contact in that office who you feel

comfortable consistently going to for answers to any

questions.

1. Contact the City Clerk's Office or appropriate agency to request a map of your district. Ask a current elected official for one of their maps. You want to think about the boundaries of your district as well as surrounding districts.

   Some districts cross into more than one city or county, so it is important to know this up front.

2. Contact the State Elections Division, and request additional information for the state district position you are seeking. Look up the job description, take notes on the current meetings of the position, and know the names and faces of those involved.

3. Print out the maps at your local printer (I recommend using a printer affiliated with a union) because it needs to be a large size so you can learn your district like the back of your hand.

   Make multiple regular size copies of the district map as well and start to learn street names, community groupings and notable landmarks.

I am going to recommend who you may need, but like the **spices in your kitchen cabinet** you do not have to use all of them at once.

This core team will turn into your family and who will likely be sacrificing the most for you.

Be clear on details and dates for deliverables, whether the work is paid or volunteer and how they can contact you with any concerns.

Always be grateful for your team and as much as

possible, do your best to make sure they always have

refreshments.

<u>10 handy options to pick up in bulk:</u>

Granola bars

Covered raisins

Mixed nuts

Donuts/ baked goods

Chips/ pretzels

Coffee/ tea

Water bottles

Energy drink packets

Fruit snacks

Popcorn

Your Kitchen Cabinet

Seasoned Salt

*Volunteer Coordinator, Administrative Assistant,
or Campaign Manager*

This is your all-purpose team player.

Some things during a campaign happen so fast, and you will need someone that is willing and able to do whatever tasks that are needed.

Keep them busy and happy for success!

Your Kitchen Cabinet

Cinnamon:

Speech Writer, Public Relations,
or Campaign Manager

When someone needs access to you and you
are not immediately available, get your
Cinnamon on the phone.

This is a person that is straightforward but has
enough spice to address campaign requests at
the executive level.

Your Kitchen Cabinet

<u>Brown Sugar</u>

*Intern, Volunteer Coordinator,
or Campaign Manager*

Everyone needs a super sweet person in their life and most importantly on their campaign.

Keep this person in the know about your recent successes and upcoming events so they can share far and wide.

They can be great at bringing on new supporters for your campaign or filling out conversations at in-person events.

Your Kitchen Cabinet

<u>Thyme</u>

*Campaign Finance Manager, Treasurer,
or Campaign Manager*

This is the person who is constantly aware of the
time and keeps you on time.

They may keep your schedule, calendar, and call-time
on track to propel your campaign forward without
missing a beat.

This is the person that supporters can go to while
you shine online and in the public! Get ready for
love and good advice, honey!

Your Kitchen Cabinet

<u>Pepper:</u>

Campaign Manager

Things can heat up during the campaign trail and so you will need someone that can be assertive in situations where it is needed.

When you need someone to grind it out and maintain the flavor of your campaign, this is your go getter!

3

Run As You Are!

**"Your story is what you have, what you will always have.
It is something to own."
~Michelle Obama~**

Running for office is for the gender

non-conforming, woman, man, partner, wife,

mother, father, sister, brother, activist, or

entrepreneur in the community.

There are many excellent organizations that can

guide you through your run for office, and many of

them I have worked with first-hand, and have

nothing but great things to say about them.

I have listed a few below:

- Vote Run Lead
- Emily's List
- Fair Fight
- GA WIN List
- Victory Fund
- New Power PAC
- Georgia Equality
- People for The American Way
- Move On

Running for office is much more demanding than you may think and holding office is an even bigger responsibility.

In the first chapter we established that you **DO** have

what it takes, and that **you've** made the decision to

represent!

<u>Who Do I Need?</u>

✔ Campaign Manager
✔ Finance Manager
✔ Volunteer Coordinator
✔ Canvass Organizer
✔ Speech Writer/Communications
✔ Inner Circle

Each of these people are important and anyone who

will work alongside them is a volunteer.

When you first begin, **you** may be filling in for all the

above, but this core team should get you started on

the road to victory.

<u>4</u>

Organization is the KEY to Justice.

"We have built permanent, independent, progressive organizing infrastructure... We want to win for our families & communities and defend those wins beyond the election cycle."
~Nse Ufot~

Get ready to be accountable to yourself and others

in a whole new way.

Keep your devices charged, your email inbox

decluttered, and your spreadsheets organized with

daily, weekly and monthly goals.

You will become a **pro** at filing campaign reports with the elections division that simplify your expenditures and donations.

Remember that you can even donate to non-profit organizations in support of their events and fundraisers for good causes!

Keep good reporting and remain transparent.

Have a **"win number"** of how many votes you need to gain by using voter file software and make a colorful board or spreadsheet to update how you're attaining it!

As it relates to canvassing, you want to make sure you know which neighborhoods have your back on day one.

You can start off by hosting canvassing events in these neighborhoods but **know** you will spend most of your time knocking doors in precincts where you need to introduce yourself (tons of cold calling and saying the same pitch over and over) to get even more support.

The goal of canvassing is to increase your name I.D and secure new voters.

Having a catchy **slogan, logo** and **stump speech** will be helpful in this key step.

Park's slogan:

"'Better Solutions For a Better Georgia"

Park's logo:

Eyeglasses because this says, "looking out for you",

"forward-thinking" and "visionary"!

(See cover of book)

Park's stump speech:

"My name is Park Cannon and I'm running for the Georgia House of Representatives. I'm a proud Georgia native, a long-time Old Fourth Ward neighbor, a life-long Democrat and a fierce reproductive justice advocate.

Georgia needs young, elected leaders who are willing to put on different lenses and view issues from multiple perspectives so that our policy making will not be out of focus.

I'm honored to have Rep. Simone Bell's endorsement in this race, but the only endorsement that REALLY matters is yours.

Park's stump speech cont'd:

We need more good jobs with good benefits, we need better transportation options, a strong ally to our kid's schools, a staunch neighborhood advocate to make sure growth is balanced and healthcare for all at the center of the campaign.

I am that candidate.

Over the next few weeks, I'm going to work everyday to earn your support, your prayers and your VOTE on or before Election Day.

Thank you!"

5

Digital Campaign Success

"You can't master your future if you're a slave to your past."
~Rihanna~

As a millennial political figure, during the time of

COVID-19, I can strongly attest to the importance

of a digital campaign strategy.

The goal of digital campaigns is to meet voters

where they are: online and on mobile devices

without neglecting your base of voters who desire to

be reached in-person.

Through email campaigns, direct messages, social media posts, and QR codes, your message can be shared and boosted on a schedule that fits your campaign life!

Remember to consider online safety by only posting 'live' when necessary, only geotagging after being on-site, and only including faces of people who agree to campaign with you. Simply ask, **"Would you be open to taking a photo with me? I might even feature it on my platform later!"**

Show positive content, behind the scenes photos of

volunteers getting ready for events and preparing

campaign materials, and address the traditional

headlines and news feed updates that you see.

●

<u>6</u>

Learn to L.A.P.

"Listen. Apply. Plan."
~Park Cannon~

When you meet neighbors in your community, I strongly encourage you to apply my L.A.P. method.

I can recall a senior resident that brought me her glasses and told me she needed them fixed. I contemplated the best way to address the situation as this was early on in my campaign career.

My brand is centered around being a visionary for a better Georgia, but also a better world. I noticed this was about more than just her literal vision, it was about her seeing and believing in my word and actions. I choose to listen, apply, and plan based on the situation at hand.

Listen

I spent no less than 1 hour hearing how she grew up in the Pittsburgh neighborhood, had seen elected officials come and go, and what she wanted to see happen in the future if I was elected.

Apply

I began to apply pressure on my team to find out where to take the glasses. I asked them to gather research on vision impairment resources, free optical clinics, and recent policies proposed or passed in the chamber I was running for.

Plan

I made a plan for staying in touch with other seniors in the area to conduct a needs assessment.

We planned how to get them back to her and acted on the references of elected officials that she mentioned in our conversation.

I will always remember this story and add it to the list of instances where even though I felt unsure on what to do, I just remembered to L.A.P.

7

Endorsements

"When campaigning, every candidate should prioritize the endorsement of the public—
meaning the people who pledge their vote over relying on endorsements from elected officials."
~State Rep. Renitta Shannon~

In my stump speech in chapter 4, I expressly seek

the endorsement of voters over organizations,

elected officials or donors in search of the voice of

the people.

Inevitably, though, interest groups will send over endorsement applications that vary in length and format, and it is up to YOU to participate in these.

Know that the statements on paper will be critical in media articles about your candidacy so no matter how informal it may seem, **your words matter.**

Tell your story and make it plain how you stand on issues. This is fun and pretty refreshing to see your policy ideas, campaign plans, and personal stories concisely written for all to see.

It can take weeks for your endorsements to come back, so be patient and supportive of their issues in the meantime to be in-the-know on how the community's needs are evolving.

8

Campaign Signs

"Yard signs don't vote."
~Any campaign manager~

Here are 3 quick tips on

how to make it worth your while

if you are going to invest in yard signs.

Many candidates fret when they see high numbers of

yard signs staked into the ground for other

campaigns and feel as though the number of yard

signs determines the number of votes to be cast.

Let me be the first to tell you, that's simply not true.

We enjoy saying that **your** campaign can determine how much a yard sign matters, based on your budget and overall outreach strategy.

We know that volunteers waving your yard signs can bring more energy to voters than a row of signs simply staked into the ground.

Hooray!

So bring the kids and fun clothing out and let your volunteers show off their personalities!

…What Matters?

Location matters—

Make your signs seen near
polling places, at coveted restaurants, in front
of community leaders' homes and in places
where it is legal.

Design matters—

Make sure your font and colors are
easy-to-read and bold enough for cars driving,
bikes riding, and people walking by to be
attracted to your signs.

Think about choosing a design where you
could use the sign multiple times.

For example, see Page 54 on how we cut off
the bottom of our 2018 sign and used it again
in 2020. Likewise, leave space to place a
sticker, in case your election goes into a
runoff—
so you can update the date!

Accessibility matters—

Make it free and easy for your supporters to gain as many signs as they would like to use for good purposes.

Use your website for yard sign requests, schedule general pickup hours that recur, and put call to actions on your robo calls to see if listeners want one!

You can say,
"Press 1 if you'd like to request a yard sign and we'll get back to you in 48 hours!"

Volunteers and/or requestors can help deliver signs to their neighborhood of like-minded voters but just keep records on their dispersal to track the utility of your signs for the overall success of your campaign.

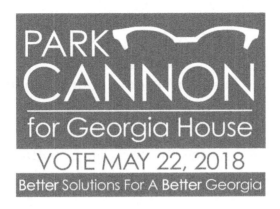

2018 yard sign

(Union bug added upon printing)

2020 yard sign

(Union bug visible on other side)

9

Call Time!

"No one has ever become poor by giving."

~Anne Frank~

It takes raising money to run for office.

I want you to be excited about running for office and see fundraising as a valuable part of the process.

Your role as an elected official will entail allocating and raising funds for public programs so do not be shy. This is like a job interview where you claim your worth and negotiate your pay—but for your campaign goals on behalf of the team and plans that rely on it.

You must be able to ask people to donate to your campaign.

Call Time: a friendly way of fundraising via the telephone.

It is necessary to be honest with yourself and others about your goals. Start goal meters and use specifics to encourage donors to give.

For example, *"I am $58 from my $500 goal, would you consider making a contribution today to support our team of volunteers knocking doors on tomorrow?"*

Or you can say, *"I was talking about my campaign with our mutual friend (insert name) and they pledged $58. They* *recommended I give you a call to see if you can match their*

$58 contribution before the close of this fundraising period on

Friday. Can you find it in your budget to join us in this race?"

What is the best way to take the edge off of

completing your first call time?

Just do it!

Call time is not that hard, and the more you do it,

the better you become.

Have your devices charged, water nearby, and

campaign plan with events open and ready to share

with potential donors during your calls.

Your consultant can prepare lists with contact

information of likely donors ahead of time so that

you can use your people skills to garner financial

support instead of gathering contacts.

Call time aids in establishing a true relationship with

your donors. You can update them on how close you

are to your goals and other election stories from the

trail. This can be fun as well as a way to connect to

their networks too! Ask them to donate and/or raise

funds on your behalf if they are unable to provide

your asking amount.

How much money do I need to raise?

The answer to this question is largely dependent upon how large your district is and the make-up of the community you plan to serve.

I've seen people win who had a bigger strategy than their budget, so it is all about how you manage the funds you raise. Use your donations wisely and be grateful for every penny you receive.

Between your own personal money, donations from friends and family, and contributions from new donors, **you will** be able to get your campaign off the ground.

How long is call time?

For effective call time I recommend at least two-hours of making consistent calls in a quiet space. Time out your calls by the minute and stick to the routine.

45 calls in 60 minutes is amazing. Remember, you can leave a concise voicemail, store their contact with a note, and plan for follow up by staying focused on this one task during call time. Emails, social media and other campaign tasks CAN wait while you dial for dollars!

Should I only call friends and family?

When you run for office you are not only representing people you know. Get used to sometimes speaking to small business owners, grassroots organizations, and introducing yourself as a candidate for office that is seeking a donation.

Who should work on my finance committee?

I recommend people from your inner circle and a trusted volunteer work on this committee.

Your finance committee needs to encourage you to help raise resources for your campaign.

What is the maximum that I can receive in donations from one person?

Keep in mind, there are limits to individual contributions so research that for your area and position.

Do not mix personal funds with campaign funds.

If someone wants to donate to your campaign account for you to purchase clothing, that might be considered unethical. Check with your treasurer before accepting unknown or unsolicited checks.

10

Justice is Before Us

"When you see something that is not right, not fair, not just, you have to speak up."
~Congressman John Lewis~

For Black and Brown communities, I understand

that many times the stigmas placed upon our culture

are unfair, I hope you know that I stand with the

mothers of Trayvon Martin, Jordan Davis, Michael

Brown, Jamarion Robinson, Rayshard Brooks,

George Floyd, Breonna Taylor, Sandra Bland, and

many others who we must make sure live forever.

Let us go forward ready to help our

communities flourish.

To law enforcement, I need to feel supported by you. The communities that we serve that are underprivileged are often treated with little to no decency.

We must change this and really make a justice system for all, and not just some.

To our healthcare workers and military members, I am asking that you also consider when minorities of race and gender come in contact with you, that they receive the same respect they should give to you. Your role in society is incomparable and I want to ask you to join in the fight for equal medical rights and access for all, no matter race or gender.

To the LGBTQ community we are a major part of the love that the world needs. Many of us have been treated as "others" when we have chosen not to identify as the options presented to us. This is a basic right, and we will remain joined in love for justice for all.

To the small business owner, non-profit organizer, or entrepreneur, you must know that it is still possible to have a profitable business in America. Establish your business so that you can stand financially independently as a candidate.

Bring the issues of all types of justice to the forefront of your campaign:

racial, economic, transit, healthcare, environmental, disability, reproductive, criminal, restorative, global and social to start a list of some that voters care to hear from you about.

This is one of the most liberating parts of running for office because it truly allows for many different viewpoints and needs to be explored and expanded based on your actions.

11

Words From My Team

"The whole is greater than the sum of its parts."
~Aristotle~

I would not be where I am today without God and

my team.

I cannot stress enough the importance of caring for

your team while on the campaign trail and beyond.

Here are a few words from my

life line team members:

~Ross H.~

Which campaign year did you work with Park on?

Her first one, in 2016!

What advice did you give Park when she ran?

She didn't need my advice!

I was just thrilled that she might represent me.

How would you describe Park on the campaign trail?

Park knows how to connect with people of all ages. She goes out of her way to care for those in the greatest need, whether it's through her relentless advocacy and legislative work or whether it's someone she just met on the street who needs some help. She's always exploring new ways she can have an impact, and she never compromises her values while still inviting discussion from all corners.

She campaigns in a way that brings in individuals and communities traditionally excluded from political processes and power. And she never stops fighting for them.

She's an inspiration, and a shining light in the politics of Georgia and the United States.

Who is this a good book for?

This is a great gift for the disillusioned non-voter looking for a reason to care.

What is one vivid memory you have with Park?

We were leaving a fundraiser for John Lewis (sometime in 2017) downtown, and as we reached the door we were stopped by a woman whom I did not recognize, but all I can say is she wore an aura of spiritual power.

She stopped Park and after an exchange of love and gratitude we all held hands and prayed as she blessed

Park, recognizing her (as I do) as an incarnation of

hope.

I'm not sure how Park felt about the whole

experience, but it felt right and very appropriate to

me!

Bless Park Cannon, now and forever!

~Brenda D.~

Which campaign year did you work with Park on?

2018

What advice did you give Park when she ran?

Not sure if I gave her wildly insightful advice.

But I believe the only thing I told her was

don't let competition or the negativity from

someone get you down.

How would you describe Park on the campaign

trail?

Park was always enthusiastic and excited on the campaign trail.

She could have personal things that bothered her, but you could never tell when she's out there meeting people, listening to their issues, and sharing all that she's doing to fight for them every day as their representative.

Regardless of the negative chatter from her competitor at the time (and past competitor from 2016) she let her track record speak for itself.

In 2018, she had strong support from a lot of people in the community.

Who is this a good book for?

This book is a great read for the American public.

Park and other activists are the reasons why GA turned Blue for the presidential and senate races.

What is one vivid memory you have with Park?

I think one vivid memory I have of Park is when I first met her.

Just seeing how she interacted with everyone she met, and how she's just very active in her community made me realize that people will someday call her

Senator Cannon

(if that's what she chooses)

I also remember Park when she fought tirelessly against the anti abortion bill in 2019.

I remember seeing her when session ended that June and I've never seen her feel so exhausted and vulnerable.

I remember thinking/praying that she didn't quit, and of course she didn't.

I think that experience could have knocked out the strongest of people. **This is why I know she's built for this and will fight tirelessly for people.**

~Shekesa M.~

Which campaign year did you work with Park on?

2016-Present

What advice did you give Park when she ran?

To continue to be herself.

Park is truly a dynamic leader. For the most part I provide creative ideas for her and she always executes them gracefully.

How would you describe Park on the campaign trail?

She's just as captivating and motivated each year.

She really cares about her people and it shows.

It's not just about her district but instead it is for the betterment of the country.

She's leap years ahead of the game.

She knows how to personally connect with people and she makes her campaign feel like she's meeting a long lost friend or family member.

Who is this a good book for?

This is a great gift for young people like her who aspire to run.

What is one vivid memory you have with Park?

Honestly, there are too many to name.

I'll say it's the "last nights" that stick out the most.

The nights where she's mentally exhausted, but continues to press forward.

Those nights when she wants to see more happen so she continues to take meetings and make calls.

She's truly an amazing community leader!

~Nathaniel G.~

Which campaign year did you work with Park on?

2020 with Congressman Kwanza Hall and former Rep. Keisha Waites

What advice did you give Park when she ran?

Saddle up and ride.

No great thing was ever achieved while awaiting a handout.

How would you describe Park on the campaign trail?

Fierce and determined.

Who is this a good book for?

The Universal Guide to Running for Office speaks to the people who didn't think they were good enough to hold an elected office.

It also speaks to our LGBTQ brothers and sisters who see acceptance in the political arena as impossible.

This book also speaks to the minorities from across the tracks who would never dream of a life in public service, but whose moral standards are crying from within demanding they rise up and stand firm in their desire to positively change their neighborhood.

What is one vivid memory you have with Park?

I saw Park walk outside barefoot.

Now, that may not be much for some, but I'm from

South Florida.

We do this regularly.

For me it solidified Park as a touchable person so to

speak.

She is relatable.

She is not above getting her hands, or her feet

dirty.

Literally.

12

Beyond Politics

"But out of limitations, comes creativity."
~Debbie Allen~

I've been dancing ballet, tap, and jazz since I was

three. Growing up in South Georgia, I was one of

few brown girls in my dance classes, and I still have

plans to open a dance studio.

As a State Representative, I am fulfilling my dream as

a decision maker at the table. I also believe I have a

civic duty to impart the dance techniques and

opportunities that I have been granted, by making

them more accessible to diverse participants.

I believe the poise I learned in ballet prepared me for

the times when I had to stand tall in the face of

injustices across the world.

The pointe shoes I wore taught me to rise above

adversity and make the voices of the true majority

heard, and the tap shoes helped me to keep the beat

when it all becomes so loud around me.

My dream for you is that **you** dream-- out loud,

overnight and into the future.

Remain hopeful for another chance to get it right

and to stand up for the change you want to see.

It is a joy to share some of the details of running for

office with you.

Let us now move into the real deal, RUNNING!

I will be with you as you take the journey forth by

way of 120 days worth of affirmations.

Legislatively

yours,

Park ♡

Instructions for 120-Day Affirmation

Step 1

Enter in the date and your personal positive affirmation for the day.

Step 2

Read my affirmation for the day.

Step 3

Repeat for each day.

Park's affirmation for the day

Day 1

I declare that my options matter.

My affirmation for

the day

Date __/__/__

_____

_____

_____

Park's affirmation for the day

Day 2

I can hold my head high in any room.

My affirmation for

the day

Date __/__/__

_____

_____

_____

Park's affirmation for the day

Day 3

I got this!

My affirmation for

the day

Date __/__/__

_____

_____

_____

Park's affirmation for the day

Day 4

I know that today is the day
for me to lead.

My affirmation for

the day

Date __/__/__

_____

_____

_____

Park's affirmation for the day

Day 5

I remember the importance of being on time.

My affirmation for

the day

Date __/__/__

_____

_____

_____

Park's affirmation for the day

Day 6

I can take care of my family
while running for office.

My affirmation for

the day

Date __/__/__

_____

_____

_____

Park's affirmation for the day

Day 7

I am enough.

My affirmation for

the day

Date __/__/__

_____

_____

_____

Park's affirmation for the day

Day 8

I know my name is worth seeing in the good news section of the paper.

My affirmation for

the day

Date __/__/__

_____

_____

_____

Park's affirmation for the day

Day 9

I know how we might be better than we are.

My affirmation for

the day

Date __/__/__

_____

_____

_____

Park's affirmation for the day

Day 10

I will cherish every moment.

My affirmation for

the day

Date __/__/__

_____

_____

_____

Park's affirmation for the day

Day 11

I will hold myself accountable.

My affirmation for

the day

Date __/__/__

_____

_____

_____

Park's affirmation for the day

Day 12

I know it is time to win.

My affirmation for

the day

Date __/__/__

_____

_____

_____

Park's affirmation for the day

Day 13

I will win without war.

My affirmation for

the day

Date __/__/__

_____

_____

_____

Park's affirmation for the day

Day 14

I stand for peace in the streets.

My affirmation for

the day

Date __/__/__

_____

_____

_____

Park's affirmation for the day

Day 15

I will hold myself accountable.

My affirmation for

the day

Date __/__/__

_____

_____

_____

Park's affirmation for the day

Day 16

I will tell the truth.

My affirmation for

the day

Date __/__/__

_____

_____

_____

Park's affirmation for the day

Day 17

I believe that the truth matters.

My affirmation for

the day

Date __/__/__

_____

_____

_____

Park's affirmation for the day

Day 18

I am happy to be here.

My affirmation for

the day

Date __/__/__

_____

_____

_____

Park's affirmation for the day

Day 19

I am ready whenever you are.

My affirmation for

the day

Date __/__/__

_____

_____

_____

Park's affirmation for the day

Day 20

I am clear on why I am doing this.

My affirmation for

the day

Date __/__/__

_____

_____

_____

Park's affirmation for the day

Day 21

I will take my time.

My affirmation for

the day

Date __/__/__

_____

_____

_____

Park's affirmation for the day

Day 22

I am patient with the process.

My affirmation for

the day

Date __/__/__

_____

_____

_____

Park's affirmation for the day

Day 23

I know that representation matters.

My affirmation for

the day

Date __/__/__

_____

_____

_____

Park's affirmation for the day

Day 24

I know that it's about time that
I treat myself.

My affirmation for

the day

Date __/__/__

_____

_____

_____

Park's affirmation for the day

Day 25

I know that everyone won't
support me and I am okay
with that.

My affirmation for

the day

Date __/__/__

_____

_____

_____

Park's affirmation for the day

Day 26

I believe that mornings are for rest.

My affirmation for

the day

Date __/__/__

_____

_____

_____

Park's affirmation for the day

Day 27

I will have that coffee.

My affirmation for

the day

Date __/__/__

_____

_____

_____

Park's affirmation for the day

Day 28

I will have that bubble tea.

My affirmation for

the day

Date __/__/__

_____

_____

_____

Park's affirmation for the day

Day 29

I am worthy of this position.

My affirmation for

the day

Date __/__/__

_____

_____

_____

Park's affirmation for the day

Day 30

I am qualified to run.

My affirmation for

the day

Date __/__/__

_____

_____

_____

Park's affirmation for the day

Day 31

I can do anything that I put
my mind to.

My affirmation for

the day

Date __/__/__

_____

_____

_____

Park's affirmation for the day

Day 32

I am the change that I want to
see in the world.

My affirmation for

the day

Date __/__/__

_____

_____

_____

Park's affirmation for the day

Day 33

I have the look.

My affirmation for

the day

Date __/__/__

_____

_____

_____

Park's affirmation for the day

Day 34

I know that they hear me.

My affirmation for

the day

Date __/__/__

_____

_____

_____

Park's affirmation for the day

Day 35

I trust in myself.

My affirmation for

the day

Date __/__/__

_____

_____

_____

Park's affirmation for the day

Day 36

I move in faith and not in fear.

My affirmation for

the day

Date __/__/__

_____

_____

_____

Park's affirmation for the day

Day 37

I can breathe through this.

My affirmation for

the day

Date __/__/__

_____

_____

_____

Park's affirmation for the day

Day 38

I know that with every move I make, I'm making moves.

My affirmation for

the day

Date __/__/__

_____

_____

_____

Park's affirmation for the day

Day 39

I want to be seen and heard.

My affirmation for

the day

Date __/__/__

_____

_____

_____

Park's affirmation for the day

Day 40

I dress for the job that I want.

My affirmation for

the day

Date __/__/__

_____

_____

_____

Park's affirmation for the day

Day 41

I look as good as I feel.

My affirmation for

the day

Date __/__/__

_____

_____

_____

Park's affirmation for the day

Day 42

I am excited for my seat at the table.

My affirmation for

the day

Date __/__/__

_____

_____

_____

Park's affirmation for the day

Day 43

I deserve my seat at the table.

My affirmation for

the day

Date __/__/__

_____

_____

_____

Park's affirmation for the day

Day 44

I claim that I will have
work-life balance.

My affirmation for

the day

Date __/__/__

_____

_____

_____

Park's affirmation for the day

Day 45

I am worthy of filling my own cup.

My affirmation for

the day

Date __/__/__

_____

_____

_____

Park's affirmation for the day

Day 46

I know that there is perfection within my imperfections.

My affirmation for

the day

Date __/__/__

_____

_____

_____

Park's affirmation for the day

Day 47

I deserve to be a voice for the future.

My affirmation for

the day

Date __/__/__

_____

_____

_____

Park's affirmation for the day

Day 48

I know how to adapt to my environment.

My affirmation for

the day

Date __/__/__

_____

_____

_____

Park's affirmation for the day

Day 49

I know that my communication will always be well received.

My affirmation for

the day

Date __/__/__

_____

_____

_____

Park's affirmation for the day

Day 50

I am doing this for the
betterment of the world.

My affirmation for

the day

Date __/__/__

_____

_____

_____

Park's affirmation for the day

Day 51

I will keep my word.

My affirmation for

the day

Date __/__/__

_____

_____

_____

Park's affirmation for the day

Day 52

I will always maintain my integrity.

My affirmation for

the day

Date __/__/__

_____

_____

_____

Park's affirmation for the day

Day 53

I will sip my tea slowly in the mornings.

My affirmation for

the day

Date __/__/__

_____

_____

_____

Park's affirmation for the day

Day 54

I am thankful for every supporter of my events- no matter how large or small.

My affirmation for

the day

Date __/__/__

_____

_____

_____

Park's affirmation for the day

Day 55

I know that my lines come from my heart not a script.

My affirmation for

the day

Date __/__/__

_____

_____

_____

_____

Park's affirmation for the day

Day 56

I can show the world who I am.

My affirmation for

the day

Date __/__/__

_____

_____

_____

Park's affirmation for the day

Day 57

I know that my experiences
are valid.

My affirmation for

the day

Date __/__/__

_____

_____

_____

Park's affirmation for the day

Day 58

I can raise enough money to
meet my goals.

My affirmation for

the day

Date __/__/__

_____

_____

_____

Park's affirmation for the day

Day 59

I will have multiple supporters
for every naysayer.

My affirmation for

the day

Date __/__/__

_____

_____

_____

Park's affirmation for the day

Day 60

I can swim through any tide.

My affirmation for

the day

Date __/__/__

_____

_____

_____

Park's affirmation for the day

Day 61

I know that the flame in me
will not be extinguished.

My affirmation for

the day

Date __/__/__

_____

_____

_____

Park's affirmation for the day

Day 62

I am a protector; I'll hold the umbrella for others when it rains.

My affirmation for

the day

Date __/__/__

_____

_____

_____

Park's affirmation for the day

Day 63

I thrive in the stillness of the early mornings and late nights to get work done.

My affirmation for

the day

Date __/__/__

_____

_____

_____

Park's affirmation for the day

Day 64

I am choosing to be happy.

My affirmation for

the day

Date __/__/__

_____

_____

_____

Park's affirmation for the day

Day 65

I am a boss because I care.

My affirmation for

the day

Date __/__/__

_____

_____

_____

Park's affirmation for the day

Day 66

I know that self-confidence is "in."

My affirmation for

the day

Date __/__/__

_____

_____

_____

Park's affirmation for the day

Day 67

I know that

self-esteem is "in."

My affirmation for

the day

Date __/__/__

_____

_____

_____

Park's affirmation for the day

Day 68

I will be remembered for my tenacity.

My affirmation for

the day

Date __/__/__

_____

_____

_____

Park's affirmation for the day

Day 69

I can take my time with important decisions.

My affirmation for

the day

Date __/__/__

_____

_____

_____

Park's affirmation for the day

Day 70

I am doing the best that I can.

My affirmation for

the day

Date __/__/__

_____

_____

_____

Park's affirmation for the day

Day 71

I wish for peace when I see
pain.

My affirmation for

the day

Date __/__/__

_____

_____

_____

Park's affirmation for the day

Day 72

I know it's only a matter of time until I am elected.

My affirmation for

the day

Date __/__/__

_____

_____

_____

Park's affirmation for the day

Day 73

I know that my smile lights up
a room.

My affirmation for

the day

Date __/__/__

_____

_____

_____

Park's affirmation for the day

Day 74

I am suited for this position.

My affirmation for

the day

Date __/__/__

_____

_____

_____

Park's affirmation for the day

Day 75

I am thriving in the present
and also focused on the future.

My affirmation for

the day

Date __/__/__

_____

_____

_____

_____

Park's affirmation for the day

Day 76

I have supporters behind me.

My affirmation for

the day

Date __/__/__

_____

_____

_____

Park's affirmation for the day

Day 77

I am ready for this journey.

My affirmation for

the day

Date __/__/__

_____

_____

_____

Park's affirmation for the day

Day 78

I seek transformation with everything I do.

My affirmation for

the day

Date __/__/__

_____

_____

_____

Park's affirmation for the day

Day 79

I can mature in the role.

My affirmation for

the day

Date __/__/__

_____

_____

_____

Park's affirmation for the day

Day 80

I know what the job description is, and I'll do more.

My affirmation for

the day

Date __/__/__

_____

_____

_____

Park's affirmation for the day

Day 81

I know this isn't in the job description but...

My affirmation for

the day

Date __/__/__

_____

_____

_____

Park's affirmation for the day

Day 82

I am agreeable to an extent.

My affirmation for

the day

Date __/__/__

_____

_____

_____

Park's affirmation for the day

Day 83

I compare myself to myself.

My affirmation for

the day

Date __/__/__

_____

_____

_____

Park's affirmation for the day

Day 84

I am passionate about
community change.

My affirmation for

the day

Date __/__/__

_____

_____

_____

Park's affirmation for the day

Day 85

I respect community elders.

My affirmation for

the day

Date __/__/__

_____

_____

_____

Park's affirmation for the day

Day 86

I sparkle because I am full of pizazz.

My affirmation for

the day

Date __/__/__

_____

_____

_____

Park's affirmation for the day

Day 87

I can "wow" a crowd by telling my story.

My affirmation for

the day

Date __/__/__

_____

_____

_____

Park's affirmation for the day

Day 88

I am worthy of being elected.

My affirmation for

the day

Date __/__/__

_____

_____

_____

Park's affirmation for the day

Day 89

I am dependable.

My affirmation for

the day

Date __/__/__

_____

_____

_____

Park's affirmation for the day

Day 90

I live for the possibility of making laws.

My affirmation for

the day

Date __/__/__

_____

_____

_____

Park's affirmation for the day

Day 91

I am intelligent.

My affirmation for

the day

Date __/__/__

_____

_____

_____

Park's affirmation for the day

Day 92

I love my life.

My affirmation for

the day

Date __/__/__

_____

_____

_____

Park's affirmation for the day

Day 93

I love running for office.

My affirmation for

the day

Date __/__/__

_____

_____

_____

Park's affirmation for the day

Day 94

I would rather keep my independence than conform.

My affirmation for

the day

Date __/__/__

_____

_____

_____

Park's affirmation for the day

Day 95

I win every day when I meet
someone new.

My affirmation for

the day

Date __/__/__

_____

_____

_____

_____

Park's affirmation for the day

Day 96

I am fueled by the thrill of justice.

My affirmation for

the day

Date __/__/__

_____

_____

_____

Park's affirmation for the day

Day 97

I believe in myself.

My affirmation for

the day

Date __/__/__

_____

_____

_____

Park's affirmation for the day

Day 98

I trust my team.

My affirmation for

the day

Date __/__/__

_____

_____

_____

Park's affirmation for the day

Day 99

I am serious about my win number.

My affirmation for

the day

Date __/__/__

_____

_____

_____

Park's affirmation for the day

Day 100

I will treat everyone in my campaign office like a special guest.

My affirmation for

the day

Date __/__/__

_____

_____

_____

Park's affirmation for the day

Day 101

I can talk with anyone about anything.

My affirmation for

the day

Date __/__/__

_____

_____

_____

Park's affirmation for the day

Day 102

I expect to be moved to action
when I hear of a new issue.

My affirmation for

the day

Date __/__/__

_____

_____

_____

_____

Park's affirmation for the day

Day 103

I will release tension so that I can be more flexible with outcomes.

My affirmation for

the day

Date __/__/__

_____

_____

_____

Park's affirmation for the day

Day 104

I can bend without breaking.

My affirmation for

the day

Date __/__/__

_____

_____

_____

Park's affirmation for the day

Day 105

I will travel to every part of
my district.

My affirmation for

the day

Date __/__/__

_____

_____

_____

Park's affirmation for the day

Day 106

I will claim my time.

My affirmation for

the day

Date __/__/__

_____

_____

_____

Park's affirmation for the day

Day 107

I am running my race not against others.

My affirmation for

the day

Date __/__/__

_____

_____

_____

Park's affirmation for the day

Day 108

I will trust in the electoral process.

My affirmation for

the day

Date __/__/__

_____

_____

_____

Park's affirmation for the day

Day 109

I will check off my

to-do list and keep it moving.

My affirmation for

the day

Date __/__/__

_____

_____

_____

Park's affirmation for the day

Day 110

I will keep it moving.

My affirmation for

the day

Date __/__/__

_____

_____

_____

Park's affirmation for the day

Day 111

I believe that there is a better way.

My affirmation for

the day

Date __/__/__

_____

_____

_____

Park's affirmation for the day

Day 112

I will run a clean campaign.

My affirmation for

the day

Date __/__/__

_____

_____

_____

Park's affirmation for the day

Day 113

I will earn my votes one at a
time.

My affirmation for

the day

Date __/__/__

_____

_____

_____

Park's affirmation for the day

Day 114

I choose how I am
represented.

My affirmation for

the day

Date __/__/__

_____

_____

_____

Park's affirmation for the day

Day 115

I choose how I am
represented.

My affirmation for

the day

Date __/__/__

_____

_____

_____

Park's affirmation for the day

Day 116

I respect different
perspectives.

My affirmation for

the day

Date __/__/__

_____

_____

_____

Park's affirmation for the day

Day 117

I do more for others because I genuinely care.

My affirmation for

the day

Date __/__/__

_____

_____

_____

Park's affirmation for the day

Day 118

I have plenty of time to accomplish my long term goals.

My affirmation for

the day

Date __/__/__

_____

_____

_____

Park's affirmation for the day

Day 119

I take initiative to refresh our government.

My affirmation for

the day

Date __/__/__

_____

_____

_____

Park's affirmation for the day

Day 120

I consider costs and benefits
when making a decision.

My affirmation for the day

Date __/__/__

_____

_____

_____

Thank you for joining me!

Please reach out to me for any inquiries on how

we can work together at:

ParkCannonConsulting@gmail.com